The Sand Bucket List

366 THINGS
TO DO WITH YOUR KIDS
BEFORE THEY GROW UP

By David Hoffman

Illustrations by Tim Kummerow

RUNNING PRESS
PHILADELPHIA · LONDON

Published by Running Press,
A Member of the Perseus Books Group

Books published by Running Press are available at special discounts for bulk
purchases in the United States by corporations, institutions, and other organizations.
For more information, please contact the Special Markets Department at the Perseus
Books Group, 2300 Chestnut Street, Suite 200, Philadelphia, PA 19103, or call
(800) 810-4145, ext. 5000, or e-mail special.markets@perseusbooks.com.

ISBN 978-0-7624- 4261-4
Library of Congress Control Number: 2011930501

E-book ISBN 978-0-7624-4503-5

9   8   7   6   5   4   3   2   1
Digit on the right indicates the number of this printing

Typography: Archer, Tamarillo, and Phoenix Chunky

Running Press Book Publishers
2300 Chestnut Street
Philadelphia, PA 19103-4371

Visit us on the web!
www.runningpress.com

To Mikey and Clare,
for knowing that the key to the mental lock
on the cupcake box was the fun of playing along

1. DANCE BAREFOOT IN A FOUNTAIN

2. TAKE THEM TO SEE YOUR
CHILDHOOD HOME

3. **Let them paint
their own room**

4. DYE YOUR HAIR WITH KOOL-AID

5. PICK AN OBSCURE NATIONAL HOLIDAY
(LIKE NATIONAL PIG DAY) AND CELEBRATE IT

6. INTRODUCE THEM TO THE BEATLES

7. SEE A MOVIE AT A DRIVE-IN THEATRE

8. FOR ONE WEEK, LIVE WITHOUT
SOMETHING YOU LOVE

9. SPEND AN ENTIRE DAY IN YOUR PAJAMAS

10. **Go to an ice cream shop and try every flavor**

11. HAVE THEM HELP WITH THE
SHOPPING BY TURNING THE THINGS
ON YOUR LIST INTO A SCAVENGER HUNT

12. LAUGH TOGETHER AT A DIRTY JOKE

13. TAKE A PICTURE OF THEM ON THE SAME DATE EVERY YEAR—IN THE SAME SPOT AND THE SAME POSE

༄

14. START A FOOD FIGHT

༄

15. INSTIGATE A PILLOW FIGHT

16. **Decide where you're going on vacation by throwing a dart at a map**

17. FOR ONE DAY, TALK ONLY IN A FOREIGN LANGUAGE (EVEN IF IT'S PIG LATIN)

༄

18. BECOME PEN PALS WITH A FAMILY IN ANOTHER STATE OR COUNTRY

19. MAKE COPIES OF PHOTOGRAPHS OF FRIENDS AND FAMILY MEMBERS —THEN PLAY CONCENTRATION USING THE PAIRS

20. TRACE YOUR FAMILY TREE

21. "PLANT" A GUMDROP TREE

22. **Jump in a swimming pool with your clothes on**

23. RESCUE A DOG OR CAT FROM A SHELTER

24. ASK THEM TO PICK A LETTER—THEN PLAN AND MAKE A MEAL WHERE EVERY DISH STARTS WITH THAT LETTER

25. DO SOMETHING WITH THEM THAT SCARES *YOU*

26. TURN A STRETCH OF SIDEWALK INTO A
CHALK-PAINTED MASTERPIECE

27. **Suck helium out of a balloon and laugh at how funny you sound**

28. FIND A GAME OR SPORT TO PLAY TOGETHER
WHERE THEY CAN LEGITIMATELY BEAT YOU

29. BUILD A GIANT GAME BOARD USING
YOURSELVES AS PLAYING PIECES

30. BOWL WITH A FROZEN TURKEY

31. GO TO THE BEACH AND BURY EACH OTHER (UP TO YOUR NECKS) IN THE SAND

32. BURY A TREASURE CHEST WITHOUT THEM KNOWING AND, MONTHS LATER, LET THEM FIND IT

33. SEND MESSAGES IN INVISIBLE INK

34. Have an indoor picnic

35. FORM A JUNKYARD BAND, WHERE ALL OF THE INSTRUMENTS ARE MADE OUT OF HOUSEHOLD ITEMS OR RANDOM THINGS YOU'VE FOUND

36. MARCH IN A PARADE

15

37. FORM A PARENT-AND-KIDS BOOK CLUB

❧

38. READ A BOOK THAT'S BEEN BANNED

❧

39. WRITE DIRTY WORDS IN THE
SAND TRAP AT A GOLF COURSE

40. **Make snow angels**

41. INSTEAD OF MAKING FACES, MAKE CHIN
FACES, AND LIP SYNC TO A MOTOWN SONG

❧

42. TRAVEL BACK IN TIME: FOR ONE WEEK-
END, LIVE, DRESS, AND EAT THE WAY PEOPLE
DID FIVE, TEN, OR TWENTY YEARS AGO

43. THROW A BACKYARD LUAU

44. PLAY IN A RAINSTORM

45. LAUNCH WATER BALLOONS

46. See who can spit their water-melon seeds the farthest

47. CREATE YOUR OWN FAMILY TRADITIONS, SUCH AS MAKING THE FIRST SATURDAY OF THE MONTH MOVIE NIGHT, OR MARKING HALF-BIRTHDAYS WITH HALF OF A CAKE

48. FIND SOMETHING NOBODY IN THE FAMILY HAS DONE—AND TRY IT TOGETHER

49. RIDE ON A ZIPLINE

❦

50. SWING, À LA TARZAN, ON A ROPE FROM TREE TO TREE

❦

51. PERFECT A TARZAN YELL

52. Scream at the top of your lungs while you ride a roller coaster with your hands above your heads

53. ENTER A PIE-EATING CONTEST

❦

54. OVERDO A GOOD THING

55. WATCH A BASEBALL GAME FROM THE DUGOUT RATHER THAN FROM THE BLEACHERS

56. SHOW THEM HOW TO "WALK THE DOG," "ROCK THE BABY," AND "GO AROUND THE WORLD"... WITH A YO-YO

57. **Rake the leaves—then jump into the pile once you're done**

58. SEE WHO CAN ROLL DOWN THE HILL THE FASTEST

59. LIE IN THE GRASS AND FIND PICTURES IN THE CLOUDS

60. GO BODY SURFING

61. GO TO A RACETRACK AND PLAY THE PONIES

62. DON'T JUST TEACH THEM TO DRIVE,
TEACH THEM TO DRIVE A STICK SHIFT

63. RIDE IN A CHERRY PICKER

64. **Cultivate an edible garden—
and fix what you grow for dinner**

65. CREATE A TIME CAPSULE, BURY
(OR HIDE) IT—THEN WAIT AND OPEN IT
FIVE OR TEN YEARS LATER

66. LISTEN TOGETHER TO
THEIR FAVORITE MUSIC

67. BUILD AN OBSTACLE COURSE IN YOUR BACKYARD

68. GO ON A DINOSAUR DIG AND HUNT FOR FOSSILS

69. AWAKEN THEM AT MIDNIGHT FOR
A LATE-NIGHT PIZZA, LEFTOVER
SPAGHETTI, OR AN ICE CREAM SODA

70. **Ice skate down a city street that has frozen over**

71. SKATE ON OLYMPIC ICE OR
SWIM IN AN OLYMPIC POOL

72. BREAK A WORLD RECORD

73. TURN YOUR HOME INTO A HAUNTED HOUSE FOR HALLOWEEN

74. HIDE A WHOOPEE CUSHION IN ONE OF THE CHAIRS AT THE THANKSGIVING TABLE

75. **Let them design and make the holiday card**

76. SEE YOUR HOUSE, THEIR SCHOOL, AND THE NEIGHBORHOOD FROM A HELICOPTER

77. EXPLORE THE BACKYARD WITH A MAGNIFYING GLASS

78. LICK THE BATTER FROM THE BOWL

79. MAKE UP LIMERICKS, AND MAKE THEM ABOUT FAMILY MEMBERS

(unless Aunt Margaret lives in Nantucket)

80. ROUND UP THE FAMILY FOR A REUNION

81. **Play Monopoly by the rules—and finish the game**

82. MAKE A MOBILE USING GELATIN MOLDS, SILVERWARE, AND OTHER KITCHEN OR COOKING UTENSILS

83. RIDE THE TEACUPS AT DISNEYLAND

84. TEACH THEM TO WRITE THANK-YOU NOTES

85. PURCHASE ONE SHARE OF
STOCK IN THEIR NAME, FROM A
COMPANY THAT INTEREST THEM

86. RENT A BOAT AND GO WATERSKIING

87. **Read a classic**

88. SUCK AN EGG INTO A BOTTLE

89. BLOW OUT AN EGG AND TURN THE
EMPTY SHELL INTO A WORK OF ART—
OR JUST CRACK IT OVER SOMEONE'S HEAD

90. EAT BREAKFAST IN BED

❧

91. GO FOR A WALK AND GET
(TEMPORARILY) LOST

❧

92. BRING THEM INTO THE BOOTH WITH YOU
WHEN YOU CAST YOUR VOTE

93. **Sing along to the car radio**

94. TAKE A LONG CAR TRIP,
EVEN IF YOU CAN AFFORD TO FLY

❧

95. AT LEAST ONCE, TRAVEL IN AN RV

96. BUY A PIECE OF VINTAGE
FURNITURE AND REFINISH IT

97. TAKE A WALK IN AN OLD CEMETERY

98. **Let them jump on
the (hotel) bed**

99. GO AROUND BLINDFOLDED FOR AN AFTERNOON

100. COMMUNICATE USING ONLY SIGN LANGUAGE

101. WATCH A SILENT MOVIE

102. DISCOVER A MOVIE YOU BOTH LOVE AND
WATCH IT TOGETHER—OVER AND OVER AGAIN

◦∞◦

103. SEE A TELEVISION SHOW
BEING TAPED OR BROADCAST LIVE

104. **Video yourself interviewing them as if they were guests on a TV news or talk show**

105. PLAY A DUET

◦∞◦

106. FEED A GIRAFFE

◦∞◦

107. SEND SECRET VALENTINES

108. SEW A HAT

109. WALK ON STILTS

110. PICK A LOCK

111. **Let them pick out YOUR clothes**

112. WATCH A BUILDING BEING BLOWN UP, DEMOLISHED, OR IMPLODED

113. SEE EVERY CITY YOU VISIT FROM THE TOP OF THE TALLEST BUILDING IN TOWN

114. RIDE AN OSTRICH, AN ELEPHANT, OR A CAMEL

115. STAND TOGETHER ON THE EDGE OF THE GRAND CANYON

116. **Visit at least one National Park**

117. GET SPRAYED BY A GEYSER

118. DIVE OFF A CLIFF INTO THE WATER

119. SHOWER UNDER A WATERFALL

120. IF POSSIBLE, VISIT THE ATLANTIC AND PACIFIC OCEANS ON THE SAME TRIP

121. BOOGIE BOARD

122. Swim with the dolphins

123. WALK ACROSS A SUSPENSION BRIDGE

124. POP A WHEELIE

125. SNOWBOARD DOWN A HALF PIPE

126. FIND YOUR WAY OUT OF A MAZE

127. CLIMB TO THE TOP OF A LIGHTHOUSE

128. BUILD A BIRDHOUSE

129. **Follow animal tracks**

130. STARE INTO THE EYE OF A TIGER (BUT BEST TO DO IT AT A ZOO)

131. ON A RAINY NIGHT, OR AROUND A CAMPFIRE, SCARE EACH OTHER WITH GHOST STORIES

132. FLY FISH

133. RUN (OR WALK) A 10K RACE

134. **Take trapeze lessons**

135. SERVE DINNER AT A HOMELESS SHELTER

136. REARRANGE ALL THE FURNITURE IN
YOUR LIVING ROOM

137. HAVE YOUR PICTURE TAKEN
IN A PHOTO BOOTH

138. TEACH THEM A BALLROOM DANCE

139. DROP A BLOCK OF DRY ICE INTO A SWIMMING POOL

140. **Finance a lemonade stand**

141. MAKE MODELING CLAY OUT OF PEANUT BUTTER, POWDERED MILK, AND HONEY—AND EAT WHAT YOU SCULPT

142. CARVE CARTOON FIGURES OUT OF A BAR OF IVORY SOAP

143. MAKE A DONATION ANONYMOUSLY

144. SQUASH A PENNY ON A RAILROAD TRACK

145. SURPRISE A NICE WAITER OR
WAITRESS WITH A *REALLY* BIG TIP

146. **Save money**

147. CREATE A LIST OF THE THINGS THEY
WANT TO DO BY A CERTAIN AGE (SUCH AS
"TWELVE THINGS TO DO BEFORE I TURN 12")
AND HELP THEM ACCOMPLISH THOSE GOALS

148. GO TO NEW YORK AND
SEE A BROADWAY SHOW

149. MAKE UP NEW LYRICS
(PERSONAL TO YOU) FOR POPULAR SONGS

150. TEACH THEM TO PLAY POKER

151. ASK THEM TO PICK A LETTER—
THEN GO TO THE LIBRARY AND CHECK
OUT A BOOK BY AN AUTHOR WHOSE
NAME BEGINS WITH THAT LETTER

152. **Play the harmonica**

153. CUT DOWN YOUR OWN CHRISTMAS TREE

154. CREATE A BUTTERFLY GARDEN

155. MAKE BALLOON ANIMALS

156. PAINT A CANVAS WITH YOUR FEET, OR
ANY BODY PART OTHER THAN YOUR HANDS

157. EAT A MEAL USING ONLY YOUR HANDS

158. **Walk on your hands**

159. MAKE BLACK AND WHITE COPIES OF
FAVORITE PHOTOS AND USE THEM TO WALL-
PAPER A ROOM OR DECORATE FURNITURE

160. PAY THE ENTRANCE FEE FOR THE
STRANGER IN LINE BEHIND YOU

161. CARVE PUMPKINS

162. LET THEM PLAN THE DINNER MENU, EVEN IF EVERY COURSE INVOLVES CHOCOLATE

163. MOLD YOUR OWN CHOCOLATES

164. GROW YOUR OWN POPCORN

165. **Milk a cow**

166. GO TO THE BEACH IN WINTER

167. GO HORSEBACK RIDING AT DAWN

168. RIDE ON A BICYCLE BUILT FOR MORE THAN ONE

❧

169. RIDE A UNICYCLE

170. **Ride the bumper cars—but only on the condition that bumping *is* allowed**

171. GIVE PIGGY BACK RIDES

❧

172. RACE GO KARTS

❧

173. HIRE A LIMOUSINE

174. USE THE DISHWASHER —NOT THE
STOVETOP OR THE OVEN—TO COOK A MEAL

175. SPEND TIME IN A PLACE
WHERE YOU ARE THE MINORITY

176. LEARN CPR

177. Slide down a fire pole

178. GO UP THE DOWN ESCALATOR

179. START A COLLECTION TOGETHER

180. HAVE A THEME DINNER (YOU CAN COOK IT YOURSELVES OR ORDER IN) WHERE THE DÉCOR AND THE DRESS MATCH THE ETHNICITY OF THE MEAL

181. THROW A GARAGE SALE TOGETHER AND DONATE THE PROCEEDS TO A CHARITY OF YOUR CHOICE

182. **Dance the hula**

183. TAKE AN OVERNIGHT TRIP (OR AT LEAST SPEND AN ENTIRE DAY) WITH EACH KID ALONE

184. RIDE A STREETCAR OR AN ELECTRIC TROLLEY

185. MASTER THE ART OF THE SOCK MONKEY

186. FOLD YOUR NAPKIN INTO A PINWHEEL

187. WRITE A LETTER TO THE EDITOR

188. **Have your palms read**

189. ON JANUARY 1, PICK SOMETHING NOT ONE OF YOU KNOWS HOW TO DO—AND LEARN HOW TO DO IT BEFORE THE YEAR IS OVER

190. DO A BACK FLIP ON A TRAMPOLINE

191. JUMP THE TENNIS NET

192. WHENEVER POSSIBLE, THROW A COIN IN A FOUNTAIN AND MAKE A WISH

193. LEAD THE CONGA LINE AT A WEDDING

194. **Climb a mountain (a real one)**

195. GET A LESS FORTUNATE KID'S LETTER TO SANTA FROM THE POST OFFICE AND BUY THAT CHILD EXACTLY WHAT THEY WANT FOR CHRISTMAS

196. SNOWMOBILE

197. JET-SKI

198. HANG A HAMMOCK IN THE LIVING ROOM

199. SEE HOW HIGH YOU CAN SWING

200. PLOT AND THROW A SURPRISE PARTY

201. **Build a sand castle**

202. CELEBRATE OTHERS' SUCCESSES

203. FINGER-PAINT—BUT YEARS AFTER
THEY ARE OUT OF KINDERGARTEN

204. CATCH SNOWFLAKES ON YOUR TONGUES

205. RENT A BILLBOARD AND LET THEM SAY ANYTHING THEY WANT

206. **Learn to juggle**

207. SEE WHO CAN SWIM UNDERWATER THE FARTHEST

208. VOLUNTEER TO BE THE ONE IN THE DUNKING BOOTH AT THE SCHOOL CARNIVAL

209. GO TO A BALLGAME ON OPENING DAY

210. HAVE YOUR PHOTO TAKEN
WITH A ROCK STAR

❧

211. SHAKE HANDS WITH THE PRESIDENT
OF THE UNITED STATES

212. **Perform a random
act of kindness**

213. BOIL A LOBSTER

❧

214. PULL OFF AN ELABORATE
PRACTICAL JOKE

❧

215. PLAY IN A SCRABBLE TOURNAMENT

216. WRITE A BOOK TOGETHER—THEN HAVE
IT BOUND AND PUBLISHED

❧

217. MAKE A STOP-MOTION ANIMATED FILM

218. **Build a tree house (one with
a trap door for a quick escape)**

219. SHOW THEM *YOUR* HIGH SCHOOL
YEARBOOK (RIDICULE ALLOWED)

❧

220. ONE DAY EACH YEAR, LET THEM SKIP
SCHOOL AND PLAY HOOKY WITH YOU

❧

221. HAVE THEM SPEND A DAY WITH YOU
AT YOUR OFFICE OR WORKPLACE

222. NURSE A SICK BIRD BACK TO HEALTH

223. EVEN IF YOU LIVE IN THE CITY, RAISE A
FEW CHICKENS FOR FRESH EGGS

224. **Make the perfect
paper airplane**

225. BAKE THE PERFECT BROWNIE

226. RUN THROUGH AN
AUTOMATED CARWASH

227. TAKE A LEAP OF FAITH

228. TELL THEM STORIES ABOUT THE DAY THEY
WERE BORN AND WHAT THEY WERE LIKE AS BABIES

❦

229. INTRODUCE THEM TO YOUR CHILDHOOD OR COL-
LEGE FRIENDS, AND LET THEM HEAR STORIES ABOUT
YOU—NO MATTER HOW EMBARRASSING THEY MAY BE

230. Skip stones on a lake

231. MAKE A SOLAR OVEN AND
USE IT TO BAKE A CAKE

❦

232. LET THEM DISASSEMBLE, DESTROY, OR DEMOL-
ISH AN OLD APPLIANCE BEFORE YOU GET RID OF IT

❦

233. DIG A HOLE TO CHINA

234. GO FOR A CAR RIDE, ASK
RANDOM PEOPLE WHICH DIRECTION
YOU SHOULD TRAVEL IN, AND SEE WHERE
THEIR SUGGESTIONS TAKE YOU

235. RIDE ALONG IN A POLICE CAR
(BUT HOPEFULLY NOT IN THE BACK)

236. **Sled down a sand dune**

237. TAKE A HIKE AT NIGHT, GUIDED
BY THE LIGHT OF THE MOON

238. TAKE A TRIP BY TRAIN

239. ENTER EVERY SWEEPSTAKES YOU RECEIVE

240. (OVER)DECORATE THE EXTERIOR AND THE FRONT YARD OF THE HOUSE FOR THE HOLIDAYS

241. **Dress as pirates and search for buried treasure**

242. MAKE REGULAR VISITS TO THE LOCAL LIBRARY

243. LEARN TO THROW YOUR VOICE

244. RAISE ANTS, BEES, OR WORMS

245. GIVE THEM FLOWERS FOR NO PARTICULAR REASON AND ON NO SPECIAL DAY

246. PRESS WILDFLOWERS IN THE SPRING— THEN IN THE MIDDLE OF WINTER FIND THE FLOWERS YOU PRESSED LAST SPRING

247. **Catch fireflies inside a jar**

248. WEAR SUNGLASSES AT NIGHT

249. SEND A MESSAGE IN A BOTTLE

250. CELEBRATE A HOLIDAY OR FESTIVAL FROM ANOTHER COUNTRY

251. SPIN A BASKETBALL ON ONE FINGER

❧

252. TURN CARTWHEELS

253. Master a really impressive card trick

254. VISIT ONE OF THE WORLD'S GREAT ART MUSEUMS

❧

255. STAY OVERNIGHT IN A MUSEUM

❧

256. SHAPE, FIRE, AND GLAZE A PIECE OF POTTERY

257. LAUGH UNTIL YOU PEE YOUR PANTS

258. WATCH EVERY EPISODE OF *I LOVE LUCY*

**259. FILM YOURSELVES EATING—
AND THEN VIEW IT BACKWARDS**

260. Let them do something that you consider dangerous

261. ENTER A SOAP BOX DERBY

262. RACE TURTLES

263. MAKE THE FAMILY VACATION
A VOLUNTEER VACATION

264. TAKE A BATH....IN MUD

265. **Race around a lake
on a paddle boat**

266. FOR ONE DAY, DO EVERY THING
BACKWARDS—EAT DINNER FOR BREAKFAST,
WEAR CLOTHES BACKWARDS,
WALK BACKWARDS, TALK BACKWARDS

267. ADMIT YOU MADE A MISTAKE

268. EAT ALL THE FROSTING OFF THE CAKE

269. THROW A TAILGATE PARTY

270. RIDE IN A MOTORCYCLE SIDECAR

271. **Toss, make, and bake your own pizza**

272. GO SEE A SEA TURTLE, A BALD EAGLE,
A WHOOPING CRANE, A GRAY WOLF, OR
ANY OTHER ENDANGERED SPECIES
AT RISK OF BECOMING EXTINCT

273. DO THE HOKEY-POKEY...ON INLINE SKATES

274. USE A POGO STICK AS A MEANS
OF TRANSPORTATION

275. SEND THEM A CARE
PACKAGE AT SUMMER CAMP

276. TAKE THEM ON A COLLEGE TOUR

277. Launch a rocket

278. DIG FOR CLAMS AND
STEAM THEM ON THE BEACH

279. WATCH "THE WIZARD OF OZ"
ON THE BIG SCREEN

280. TEACH AN OLD DOG A NEW TRICK

281. EAT WEIRD FOODS

❧❦❧

282. LISTEN TO A LIVE PERFORMANCE OF
MOZART OR BEETHOVEN, OUTDOORS

283. **Star gaze**

284. WATCH AN ECLIPSE

❧❦❧

285. COACH THEIR TEAM

❧❦❧

286. ENTER A DANCE CONTEST

287. RELEASE BALLOONS IN AN UNEXPECTED PLACE

288. COOK DINNER IN THE FIREPLACE

289. ROAST MARSHMALLOWS AND MAKE S'MORES

290. **Win a giant stuffed animal by playing a carnival game**

291. USING BLANKETS AND SHEETS, MAKE A FORT UNDER THE DINING ROOM TABLE

292. HARVEST YOUR OWN FRESH HONEY

293. IN THE WEEKS BEFORE YOU
REMODEL OR REPAINT, LET THEM
DRAW ALL OVER THE WALLS

294. MAKE A GINGERBREAD
HOUSE FROM SCRATCH

295. **Pan for gold**

296. POP CORN WITH THE LID OFF

297. SERVE DINNER—ON THE ROOF

298. START A FASHION TREND

299. BID ON—AND BUY—SOMETHING
AT A LIVE AUCTION

300. PRETEND YOU DON'T SPEAK ENGLISH

301. LEARN TO COUNT TO 10
IN TEN DIFFERENT LANGUAGES

302. **Find a pond where you can feed and watch the ducks**

303. COMB THE BEACH FOR GLASS AND SHELLS

304. TEACH THEM YOUR FAVORITE SPORT

305. BE AN EXTRA IN A MOVIE

⊱✦⊰

306. GO DUMPSTER DIVING

307. **Perform on a public street and pass the hat when you're done**

308. GO AWAY FOR THE WEEKEND WITH NO PLANS, NO ITINERARY, AND NO RESERVATIONS

⊱✦⊰

309. VISIT ALL FIFTY STATES

⊱✦⊰

310. VISIT ALL SEVEN CONTINENTS

311. FIND THE OPPORTUNITY TO LIVE IN A FOREIGN COUNTRY

❧

312. STAY UP ALL NIGHT AND WATCH THE SUN RISE

313. **Go river rafting and shoot the rapids**

314. HAND OUT FULL-SIZE CANDY BARS AT HALLOWEEN

❧

315. FACE PAINT USING PUDDING (OR FACE PLANT INTO A BOWL OF PUDDING)

❧

316. TOUCH YOUR TONGUES TO YOUR NOSES

317. BUILD A SNOWMAN

318. BUY THE BEST SEATS IN THE HOUSE FOR
A CONCERT, PLAY, OR SPORTING EVENT

319. **Snag a major
league baseball**

320. ORGANIZE A NEIGHBORHOOD OLYMPICS
OR A "TOUR DE NEIGHBORHOOD" BIKE RACE

321. EAT DIM SUM FOR BREAKFAST

322. HOLD A SÉANCE

323. SHARE A PRIVATE JOKE

324. BLOW A FOGHORN

325. **Blow a bubble the size of your head**

326. LEAVE COOKIES AND MILK FOR SANTA

327. HAVE YOUR PHOTO TAKEN WITH SANTA, LONG AFTER EVERYONE HAS STOPPED BELIEVING

328. RENT A JUKEBOX AND THROW A DANCE PARTY JUST FOR THE FUN OF IT

329. TIE STRING BACK AND FORTH
ACROSS A ROOM AND CRAWL
THROUGH, TRYING NOT TO TOUCH IT

330. CRACK A SECRET CODE

331. **Order room service**

332. GO DOWN IN A SUBMARINE

333. MAKE CANDLES

334. TOUR A CANDY FACTORY

335. BUILD A HOUSE OF CARDS

336. SHOOT CRAPS

337. **Master a miniature golf course and win a free game on the 18th hole**

338. WATCH A BABY BE DELIVERED

339. GO TO A SENIOR CENTER TO
READ WITH THE RESIDENTS

340. MAKE DINNER USING RECIPES FOUND
IN THEIR GRANDMOTHER'S COOKBOOK

341. HANG SPOONS FROM YOUR NOSES

342. MAKE A THERMOS FULL
OF HOT CHOCOLATE AND WATCH
FIREWORKS ON NEW YEAR'S EVE

343. **Build a tire swing**

344. RIDE IN A BLIMP

345. SOLVE THE RUBIK'S CUBE

346. LEARN HOW TO USE A COMPASS

347. SET UP AND MAINTAIN AN AQUARIUM

348. **Go snorkeling**

349. SECRETLY FREEZE GIRL SCOUT THIN
MINTS IN MARCH—THEN SURPRISE THEM
WITH THOSE COOKIES IN OCTOBER

350. BARGAIN FOR A DEAL AT A FLEA MARKET

351. MAKE ORIGAMI
OUT OF A DOLLAR BILL

352. LEARN TO WHISTLE (LOUDLY)
WITH TWO FINGERS

❦

353. INVENT A NEW FLAVOR OF ICE CREAM
—THEN MAKE IT YOURSELVES

354. **Make a kite and fly it in a windstorm**

355. WRITE YOUR NAME—OR LEAVE YOUR
HANDPRINTS—IN WET CEMENT

❦

356. PLAY FLASHLIGHT TAG,
AFTER DARK, ON A SUMMER NIGHT

357. ONCE A DAY, FOR THIRTY DAYS,
GO FOR A WALK ALONG THE SAME ROUTE
AND SEE HOW IT CHANGES WITH TIME

358. **Pitch a tent and sleep outside in the back yard**

359. CATCH MOONBEAMS

360. PLAN A PROGRESSIVE DINNER
PARTY WITH YOUR NEIGHBORS,
WHERE EVERYONE GOES FROM HOUSE
TO HOUSE, ENJOYING A DIFFERENT
COURSE OF THE MEAL AT EACH HOME

361. SLOW DOWN

362. KEEP A FAMILY LIST OF THINGS YOU ARE GRATEFUL FOR

363. **Take a family portrait where everyone is wearing Groucho glasses**

364. TRADE PLACES

365. SAIL INTO THE SUNSET

366. COUNT UP EVERYTHING IN THIS BOOK THAT YOU'VE ALREADY DONE